Mel Bay's

Appalachian Folk Songs

for Piano & Voice
(with Guitar Chords)

by Richard L. Matteson, Jr.

Featuring ballads and songs from the
collection of Dr. Maurice Matteson

Illustrations by Charla Barnard

Visit us on the Web at http://www.melbay.com — E-mail us at email@melbay.com

Foreword

After writing *An Appalachian Christmas* for Mel Bay Publications, Bill Bay suggested I follow with another piano and voice book on Appalachian folk songs.

Most of the folk songs in this book come from the collection my grandfather, Maurice Matteson, recorded in the 1930's. He was possibly the first collector to find such now popular tunes as *Tom Dooley* and the *Wildwood Flower*.

I would like to thank Bill Bay and Mel Bay Publications for their encouragement and willingness to publish this book.

Also thanks to Mrs. Zoraya Mendez-Decosmis, print licensing Manager at G. Shirmer, for allowing me permission to use the melodies of several selections from my grandfather's book, *Beech Mountain Folk-Songs and Ballads*.

The goal of this book is to present folk melodies for piano solo that are simple yet interesting. The melody line is included in each solo along with the lyrics so that the vocalist can double the melody if the vocal is desired. The harmonies are generally traditional I, IV, V progressions although some spice is added to create variety.

Several of the tunes are arranged by my grandfather and in several others I simply kept his harmonies and added the melody line.

To give you a variety of arrangements I've enlisted the aid of several fine pianists and arrangers. Thanks to Mrs. Ann Matteson (my mother), Anthony Russell, Rebekah Fishel and Cindy Long whose arrangements also appear in this book.

Richard L. Matteson, Jr.

Contents

About the Author

Richard L. Matteson, Jr. is nationally recognized for his books, magazine articles and workshops on American folk music. He is President of the Piedmont Guitar Society and gives regular workshops and performances at the Merle Watson Memorial Festival in Wilkesboro, NC and the Chet Atkins Appreciation Society Convention in Nashville.

His other Mel Bay books, *Appalachian Folk Songs for Acoustic Guitar, Early American Hymns for Acoustic Guitar, American Fiddle Tunes for Acoustic Guitar* and *An Appalachian Christmas for Piano and Voice* reflect his deep interest in American folk music.

His mother, Ann S. Matteson, whose arrangements appear in this volume, is President of the Maryland State Piano Teachers Association and his grandfather, Maurice Matteson, collected most of the folk tunes for this book in the 1930's.

Richard L. Matteson, Jr. directs guitar studies at Winston-Salem State University and Salem College and is a full-time music teacher at Pearson Music Co. in Winston-Salem, NC.

Dedication

Dr. Maurice J. Matteson was my grandfather. He died over 30 years ago in Beaufort, South Carolina. Much of his career was dedicated to collecting, arranging and performing traditional American folk songs and especially Appalachian folk songs.

Most of the tunes and lyrics in this book were gathered from my grandfather's manuscripts collected in the 1930's. It is an honor for me to have unearthed new gems from his tattered manuscripts to preserve for future generations.

In the early 1930's while Maurice Matteson was the director of the School of Music at the University of South Carolina, he spent his summers directing the vocal work at the Southern Appalachian Music Camp in Banner Elk, North Carolina. A chance meeting with folk song collector Mellinger Henry in the North Carolina mountains would change his life (see *Wanted!-Mountain Music*).

With the aid of Henry, Matteson began his lifelong quest to collect, arrange and perform ballads and folk songs. His collection from the Banner Elk area resulted in the G. Schirmer book, *Beach Mountain Folk-Songs and Ballads*. Several of these tunes are included here as well as several unpublished songs.

In 1938 Professor Maurice Matteson had just come to New York City from a song collecting trip in the Southern Appalachian Mountains. There he met Frank Warner and showed him his dulcimer made by Nathan Hicks of Beech Mountain, North Carolina. Warner later visited Hicks and collected an unknown song, "Tom Dooley" from Frank Proffit, Hicks' son-in-law. Later the song became a huge hit for the Kingston Trio. There exists an earlier version of "Tom Dooley" in my grandfather's manuscripts.

As first president of the Southern Folklife Society, he was instrumental in publishing *The Southern Folklore Quarterly*. For this impetus towards preservation of American Folk materials and his published material and folk lectures, he received the honorary Doctor of Music Degree from the Sherwood Music School, Chicago. My grandfather associated with such noteworthy song collectors as John Jacob Niles, Frank Warner, W.C. Handy, Bascom Lundsford, John Powell, Mrs. John Buchanan and Percy Grainger.

The Maurice Matteson Music Collection is displayed at the University of South Carolina Library in Columbia, South Carolina.

The Appalachians: Mountaineers and Their Music

The Mountains and Their People

The Appalachian mountain range covers over 110,000 square miles and includes about one-third the area of the states of Georgia, Alabama, North and South Carolina, Tennessee, Kentucky and Virginia. Parts of Maryland and Pennsylvania outline the Appalachians' northern reach.

These hardy settlers immigrated from the British Isles and made their way down the Daniel Boone Trail and into the remote accesses of the Appalachians. Isolated from the world by the mountains' rugged terrain, the songs they bought from their homelands across the ocean were passed from generation to generation. Ballads that had disappeared in England over two hundred years ago are still found in a pure form in the mountains.

The early song collectors (1910–1930) found the mountaineers unaffected by the modernizations of the cities. The roads were poor, electricity, television, radio, telephone lines were slow to make their way into these rocky regions. Most of the mountaineers were God-fearing souls who lived off the land by raising crops and hunting in the forests. They owned their land but had little money and bartered for clothing and goods they couldn't make or grow.

Song Collectors and Mountain Songs

When Francis James Child published his lifetime of research, *English and Scottish Popular Ballads*, in the late 1800's, he didn't realize that a great wealth of ballads and folk songs existed in the Appalachian region. Nearly a third of Child's collection containing 305 distinct folksongs and ballads were later found in Appalachia.

Cecil Sharp, one of the leading English folklorists and collectors, came to the United States during the First World War and was persuaded by Mrs. Campbell to edit her book of Appalachian mountain songs. He became so excited by the songs she'd found that he quit his lecturing circuit and spent the next three years collecting Appalachian folksongs.

Sharp's book, *English Folk Songs of the Southern Appalachians*, was published in 1917 and contains 273 separate songs and 968 tunes. It is the definitive volume of Appalachian folksongs and opened the door for other collectors to follow.

Ballads and Folk Songs

Although the difference between a *ballad* and folk song is often arbitrary, a ballad is a narrative song that tells a story while a *folk song* is a more personal and emotional expression usually dealing with love or sorrow.

The Music

The music found in the mountains is usually modal and frequently hexatonic (six-note) or pentatonic (five-note). The third of the scale when present is sometimes lowered and used along with the major third in the same song.

The songs Cecil Sharp and the early collectors heard were usually unaccompanied.

Sharp found just one guitar and several fiddles but other folk instruments, such as the lap dulcimer, were used.

The folk songs and ballads were passed down from generation to generation. As the songs were passed, changes were made not only in the song melodies but in the lyrics as well. Different songs emerged from existing songs that had new variations of the original's lyrics and melodies.

Today, many of the old ballads and songs have disappeared or are vanishing. It is important that records of these ballads and songs be kept for future generations.

The Modes

The modes: My definition of a mode is a set number of steps between the degrees of a scale. In the pentatonic modes, the interval between two of the degrees is one and a half steps.

Cecil Sharp and other folk musicologists have created a system of modes to identify folk songs. The modes commonly used in folk songs and hymns are found in the chart below.

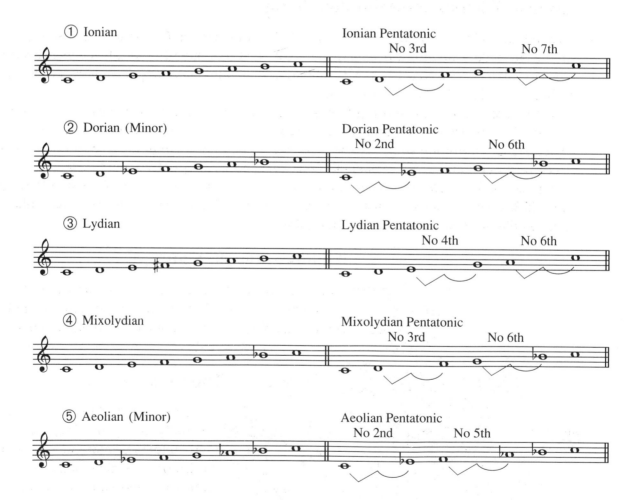

Wanted! Mountain Music

by

Maurice Matteson

In the western tip of North Carolina within seven miles of the Tennessee line, a great shaggy mountain lifts up its head from a cross range of the Blue Ridge and Appalachian Mountains. Not as high as Grandfather Mountain towards the south, to which it says "good morning" each day, nor as imposing as Roan Mountain to the west, which keeps a sentinel watch over the Tennessee line, this mountain stretches for seven or eight miles, ridged with peaks called "The Pinnacles." Thus Beech Mountain is the sky outline for miles on all sides.

If one climbs The Pinnacles, one may look to the north for thirty miles or more into Virginia. Here under one's sight lie undulating ridges of lesser ranges; while to the east, one looks with a comparatively unrestricted view for fifteen miles to the Blowing Rock region. All of this magnificent vista, until recently completed good roads, was accessible only to the most seasoned mountain traveler and adventurer.

Sitting one day this past summer on the velvety green terrace at Pinnacle Inn, a charming little hotel built on English lines, I was engaged in lazily surveying the far flung reaches of Beech, over which floated gossamers of clouds. The Inn and its beautiful grounds comprise the greater part of the little town of Banner Elk, N.C., which nestles at the gap leading from Boone, N.C. on one side and Elizabethton, Tennessee on the other.

Sitting in the deck chair near me and engaged in the same pleasurable pastime was a portly gentleman of whom I inquired, "Why do you suppose they call this mountain Beech?"

"Well," at last he ventured, all the while puffing on a long odorous cigar, "largely on account of the magnificent specimen of beech trees which you may see in groves on the slope of the mountain." "Incidentally," he said, "all of the beeches in this region of western North Carolina are becoming affected by the blight which has nearly eradicated the beautiful beech groves of Pennsylvania."

Then he asked, "Don't you know these mountains?" After informing him that I was enjoying my first mountain vacation while away from my university classes, he shifted in his chair and suddenly barked, "Do you know anything about ballads?" Somewhat taken by surprise I confessed my ignorance of any save *Barbara Allen*.

He drew closer and looked me in the eye and said, "If you want to do something worthwhile musically then you could add to the world of literature by searching the recesses of Beech Mountain and its vicinity for fragments and variants of the Old English and Scottish ballads and correctly record their tunes. In the coves and slopes of Beech Mountain are sheltered the homes of mountaineers who for generations have known and sung the folk songs of the past in almost perfect preservation."

"Scholars have now agreed," continued he, "that the collecting of words alone without the tunes as well is only half worthwhile."

I then learned that this genial and unusually interesting person was none other than Mellinger Edward Henry, who has often contributed to the *Journal of American Folklore,* and whose books on ballads and folk songs provide a great fund of information to American literature.

It was through this casual conversation with Mr. Henry that I started what proved to be one of the most exciting summer activities of my life: running down folk tunes, folk songs and ballads.

Through Mr. Henry's assistance, I came to know many of the "first families in America" and recorded many of the tunes of this region. The result of the ballad collection is to be published under the title, *Beech Mountain Ballads.* I have also discovered numbers of interesting folk tunes and verse, many of which have not become generally known. Among the more unusual is entitled "Sinful to Flirt."

Sinful to Flirt (see page 42)

Oh, they say it is sinful to flirt,
Oh, they say that my heart is made of stone;
Oh, they say to speak to him kindly,
Or else leave the poor boy alone.

Oh, they say he is only a boy,
But I am sure he is much older than me,
And if they would leave us alone,
I'm sure much happier we would be.

I remember the night when he said,
That he loved me far more than his life,
He kissed me and called me his pet,
And asked me to be his wife.

"Oh Willie," I said with a smile,
"I am sure that I'll have to say no."
He took my hand for a while,
And said, "Goodbye, I must go."

"Oh darling," I said, "I am sure,
Your heart is made of stone."
He took a white rose from my hair,
And left me standing there.

Next morning poor Willie was dead,
He was drowned in a pond by the mill.
In the pure blessed water so fair,
That flows from the banks of the hill.

His eyes were forever closed,
And damp was his bright golden hair,
And close to his pale lips he held,
The white rose he took from my hair.

Oh Willie, my darling come back,
I will ever be faithful to you;
Oh Willie, my darling come back,
I will ever be faithful and true.

This charming lyric was sung for me by Mr. Nathan Hicks, a sturdy mountaineer of Sugar Grove, Beech Mountain. He sang very simply, with no trace of embarrassment, his blue eyes sparkling with the unconscious zest of the true artist.

The case of Mr. Hicks is an interesting one. Through Edward Tufts, a young boy of Banner Elk, I heard of Nathan Hicks and his reputation as a ballad singer and also a maker of mountain dulcimers, which in his mountain drawl becomes *dul-ci-moor*.

One evening about sunset, we decided to take a journey to see Mr. Hicks. Young Edward told me that since it was only a half mile off the main road we could get there in half an hour. I shall never forget the climb from McGill Gap where we turned off to ascend Beech Mountain. The road became gradually worse and as the shadows of the evening lengthened over the mountainside, I became apprehensive about getting back before dark.

Edward and his companion assured us that it was only a few minutes ride further until we reached Woods Man Cove where Hicks was supposed to be living. Imagine our great consternation when we, after turning several more hairpin curves, discovered from a callow youth trudging in the evening dusk along the road that Hicks had moved.

I have observed that expeditions having been attempted and seemingly failed could be terminated in an *about face* and going home. Here was one case where this was not possible because the mountain road had become so narrow. We had climbed until there was a sheer drop of hundreds of feet on one side of the road with rocks and boulders ascending hundreds of feet on the other! My car was a long one and it was impossible to turn back.

The two boys and I held a consultation and decided we might as well go on to where Hicks had moved, "about a couple of miles further on." So we started ahead, I with great trepidation and the boys, quite accustomed to mountain roads and escapades of all kinds, urging me on.

The road became more and more difficult to travel and the rocks over which we passed larger and larger. At this point dusk had turned into evening and it had become necessary to put on the car lights to see where we were going. Again I surely would have turned back if it had been possible to do so.

After rounding a curve, a view, such as I shall never forget, greeted our eyes. We had encircled the eastern end of Beech and had emerged on the north side where the final glow of the setting sun was roseately coloring the western clouds. Night itself emerged from the east over the range of mountain peaks, visible for miles to the north. The vastness of that majestic and breath-taking sight will always remain as one of my treasured memories.

At this juncture I refused to go farther and insisted that young Edward climb the mountain slope to a little lighted home several hundred yards up and inquire if we were anywhere near Nathan Hicks. By the time he returned night had descended but a ray of helpfulness was the young moon which made its appearance from behind us over the mountain top.

Edward informed us that Mr. Hicks was only a half a mile farther on. In case you don't believe a half a mile is a long ways, try any of the mountain half miles. It means up, and over, and around, and anything else you would like to add.

In the course of a half hour, we reached a stone barn built right at the side of the road and down the slope we saw a light glimmering. Again the boys were dispatched to see if this was Nathan's cottage. This proved to be the case and at last, after the perilous journey of an hour and a half, we glimpsed Mr. Hicks.

He very cordially invited us to stay and spend the night but I had entirely too much nerve strain to accept. After promising to come to Banner Elk and sing for me, he opened the barn doors (which might be a good one for Ripley) and believe it or not we backed the car into the barn and thus were able to turn around.

When he sang for me in Banner Elk, he accompanied himself on the dulcimer, a three-stringed fiddle-like instrument, which he tuned in octaves and a fifth. Upon this he created a remarkable accompaniment, at times pulsating with rhythm and at other times reflecting the pathos of the lyrics he was singing.

What he accomplished so simply is not so easy. I can testify that I have practiced the dulcimer for months and have not mastered this instrument.

Two other songs contributed by Nathan Hicks were *Once I Knew a Little Girl* and *Away Out on the Mountain*. (For the music and lyrics see *Once I Knew a Little Girl* page 34 and *Away Out on the Mountain* page 24.)

Another unusual folk song was contributed by Mrs. Lena Turberfield of Elk Park, N.C. Mellinger Henry had heard of the gifted singing of Mrs. Turberfield and her family, and we journeyed together one morning down the mountain to Elk Park. On the outskirts of town in a very humble cottage we found the entire family; Mrs. Turberfield, Mrs. Bragg and Miss Sabra Hampton, the men of the family and many offspring.

It might to interesting to the uninitiated how we went about collecting a folk tune or ballad. Mr. Henry journeyed in first while Mrs. Henry and my five-year-old son and I waited in the car. While we waited Mr. Henry approached them with remarks regarding the weather, an unusual rainy season, and threw in a reminder that he had sent them a note that he might call upon them at some time in regard to folk songs and ballads. Having established himself in standing, he waved to us and we felt at liberty to come in.

With the kindness and hospitality that is characteristic of all the mountain families, there was a great adjustment of seating arrangements and a hurried call for more chairs to be brought on the porch which was already overtaxed with the family itself. After many rearrangements we were all seated in cane bottom chairs which would undoubtedly be the envy of many an antique collector.

At last we were ready to proceed with further conversation. I was identified as the musical member of the party with Mrs. Henry as her husband's great helper in the collecting of tunes and folklore on other expeditions. When I attempted to arrange my son on the porch steps, Miss Hampton suggested, "let 'em play with the least of 'em."

Mr. Henry, seeing my blank look, explained, "She meant the smallest of the many children playing in the yard."

So having disposed of Richard and the "least of 'em," we were ready to swing the conversation to the point of the visit. Mrs. Henry asked the three sisters if they knew a song about the King of France; referring to one of the many Child ballads which, as yet, has not been found in this country. Only blank states greeted her attempt.

Mr. Henry ventured, "Do you know *The Brown Girl?*" This is one of the favorite folk songs of all the mountain sections of the Carolinas and Virginia. Again they seemed not to understand what we meant. Mr. Henry had suggested *The Brown Girl* because he knew that most mountaineers knew that particular folk tune. But the mountaineers are very secretive and one must establish complete confidence before it is possible to gain any information from them.

By strange insight, I recalled the first verse and tune of *The Brown Girl* as I had collected it from Mr. Hicks, so I burst into song with this lyric. Instantly we were all on safe ground as the three sisters faces brightened and they assured us they knew that one.

Under Mr. Henry's skillful guidance, they were soon singing many of the familiar songs. Every now and then we had to switch them from mountain tunes they had heard on records or over the radio. We soon managed to get them to understand that we weren't interested in radio or record recordings.

At this juncture an aged neighbor, well over eighty, seeing the strange car at the Braggs, came down the mountain road to investigate. Her coming occasioned another hectic period of seating rearrangement. Ten minutes were taken to seat this old lady, whose name escapes me. After finding out what we were trying to get, she claimed that there were many fine tunes that they had not sung yet. She suggested *Bolakin* which at first we did not recognize as one of the Child ballads; *Lamkin*.

Soon they were busy singing the verses to this fine ballad which proved to be one of the finds of the morning visit. From Mrs. Turberfield I have possession of the lyrics to *The Jealous Lover* also named *Blue-Eyed Ella* (see page 30) and *Shady Valley*.

As they sang I was busy getting the musical notation of these ballads and songs while Mr. and Mrs. Henry were attempting to get the words. Often we weren't able to notate these folk songs in one singing so we would encourage the singers to repeat the stanzas and melodies by joining with them. They declared to have heard both *Fair Eleanor* and *Shady Valley* from their mother who learned them from her grandmother.

So in every case, a sense of comradeship must be established before the preservers of folk tunes and ballads are willing to sing for you.

The Cuckoo

Text and Air from Mrs. Joseph A. Gaines
Glasgow, KY   Aug. 30, 1936
Collected by Maurice Matteson
Arranged by Ann and Richard L. Matteson, Jr.

The Old Shoemaker *

Text and Air from the singing of Mrs. Jos. A. Gaines
Glasgow, KY   Aug. 30, 1936
Collected by Maurice Matteson
Arranged by Ann and Richard L. Matteson, Jr.

1. I'm an old shoe-mak - er by my trade— just late-ly be - come a free-man, ___ and all I want in this wide world, is just to gain a wo-man.

Tom fal di id-dle i dag, Tom fal di lar - ro ___ Tom fal di id - dle i day, oh Kate you are ___ a dear - o. ___

* See song notes for additional verses.

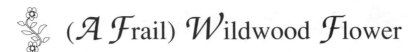

(A Frail) Wildwood Flower

Text and Air from Edith Robbins
Banner Elk, NC   Aug. 5, 1933
Collected and Arranged by Maurice Matteson

1. I'll twine with my ring, made of ra-ven black hair, A rose ____ so red and a lil-y so fair, The myr-tle so green with its em-er-ald hue and pale ____ Er-me-ta with eyes of dark blue.

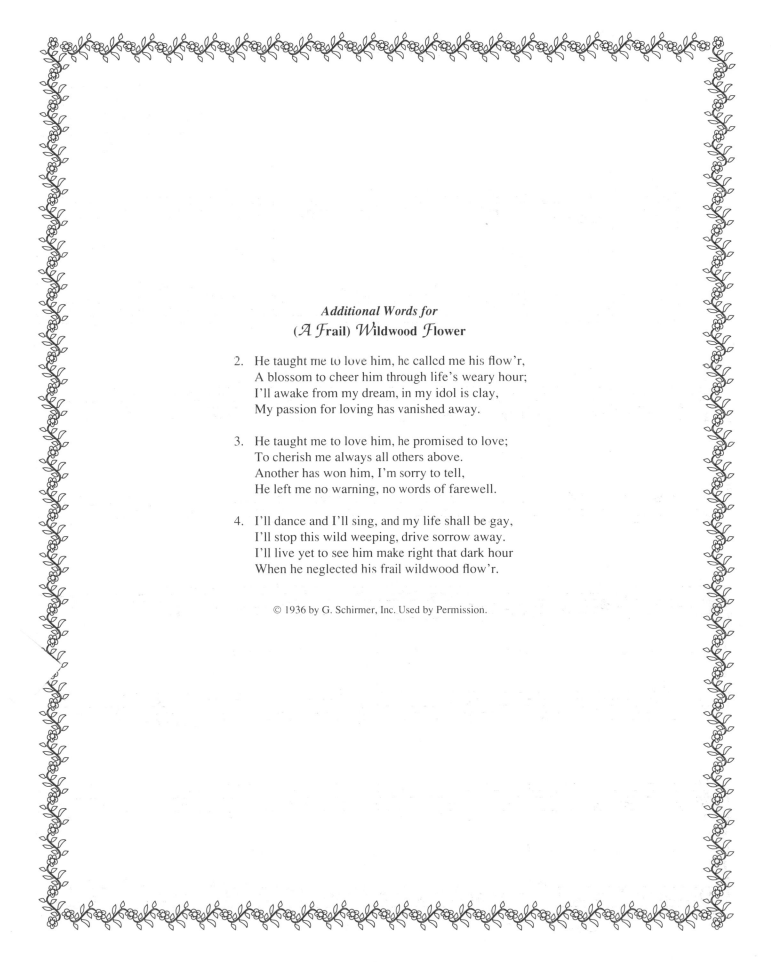

Additional Words for
(*A* Frail) *W*ildwood *F*lower

2. He taught me to love him, he called me his flow'r,
    A blossom to cheer him through life's weary hour;
    I'll awake from my dream, in my idol is clay,
    My passion for loving has vanished away.

3. He taught me to love him, he promised to love;
    To cherish me always all others above.
    Another has won him, I'm sorry to tell,
    He left me no warning, no words of farewell.

4. I'll dance and I'll sing, and my life shall be gay,
    I'll stop this wild weeping, drive sorrow away.
    I'll live yet to see him make right that dark hour
    When he neglected his frail wildwood flow'r.

The Rosewood Casket

Text from Nathan Hicks
Air from Mrs. Edward Tufts,
Banner Elk, NC   July 25, 1933
Collected by Maurice Matteson
Arranged by Cindy E. Long

Intro **Sweet, Expressive**

mf

Verse

1. There's a

lit - tle rose - wood cas - ket ___ Sit-ting on a mar - ble stand, With a

mf *sim.*

pack - age of love let-ters ___ Writ-ten _ by my true love's hand. 2. Will you

(Vocal 8va lower. . .)

get them now dear sis - ter? ___ Will you read them o'er to me? For oft-

times　I've tried　to　read them ＿＿＿＿ But for　tears　I could　not　see.

Ending

Additional Words for
The Rosewood Casket

3. Read these precious lines so slowly
   That I may miss not even one,
   For the cherished hand that wrote them—
   His last work for me is done.

4. Tell him that I never blamed him,
   Though he's proved to me untrue;
   Tell him that I'll never forget him,
   Till I bid this world adieu.

5. You have finished now, dear sister;
   Will you read them o'er again?
   While I listen to you read them,
   I will lose all sense of pain.

6. While I listen to you read them,
   I will gently fall asleep—
   Fall asleep to wake with Jesus.
   Oh, dear sister, do not weep.

7. When I am dead and in my coffin,
   And my shroud's around me bound,
   And my little bed is ready
   In the cold and silent ground.

8. Place his letters and his locket—
   Place together o'er my heart;
   But that little ring he gave me,
   From my finger never part.

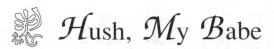

Hush, My Babe

Appalachian Folk Carol
Traditional Melody, Text by Watts
Arranged by Richard L. Matteson, Jr.

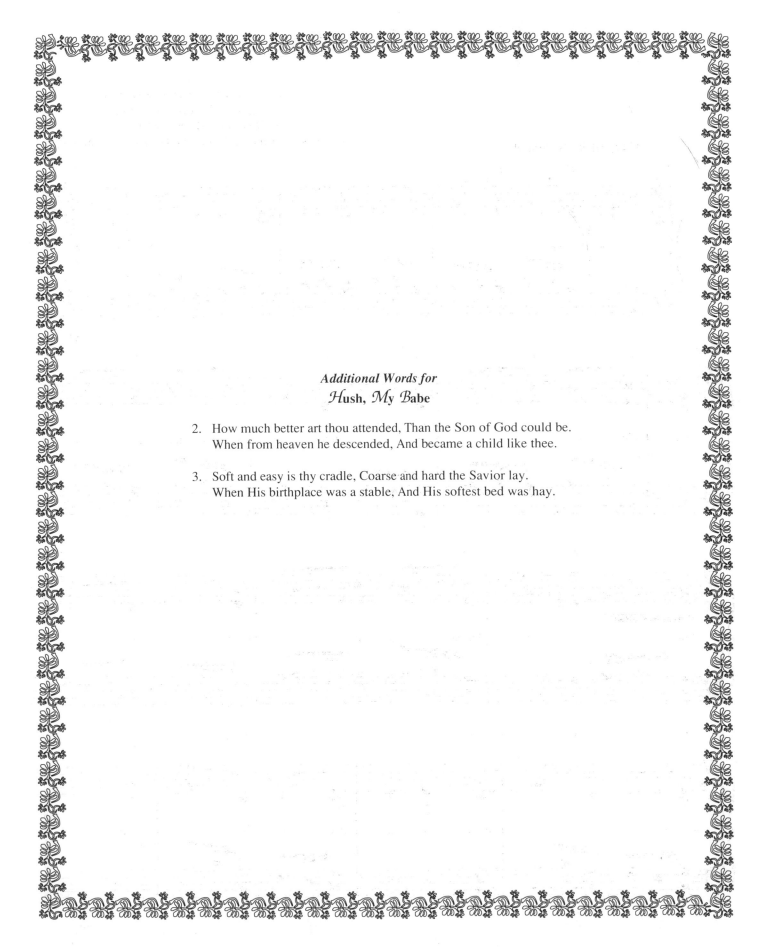

Additional Words for
Hush, My Babe

2. How much better art thou attended, Than the Son of God could be.
    When from heaven he descended, And became a child like thee.

3. Soft and easy is thy cradle, Coarse and hard the Savior lay.
    When His birthplace was a stable, And His softest bed was hay.

Old Maid's Song

Text and Air from Mollye Wilcox
Berea, KY   Aug. 17, 1933
Collected by Maurice Matteson
Arranged by Rebekah Fishel and Richard L. Matteson, Jr.

Gaily with Movement

Lyrics:

An old man came to my house, He would not tell his name. I know he came a-court-in' but seemed to be a-shamed, Oh he seemed to be a-shamed.

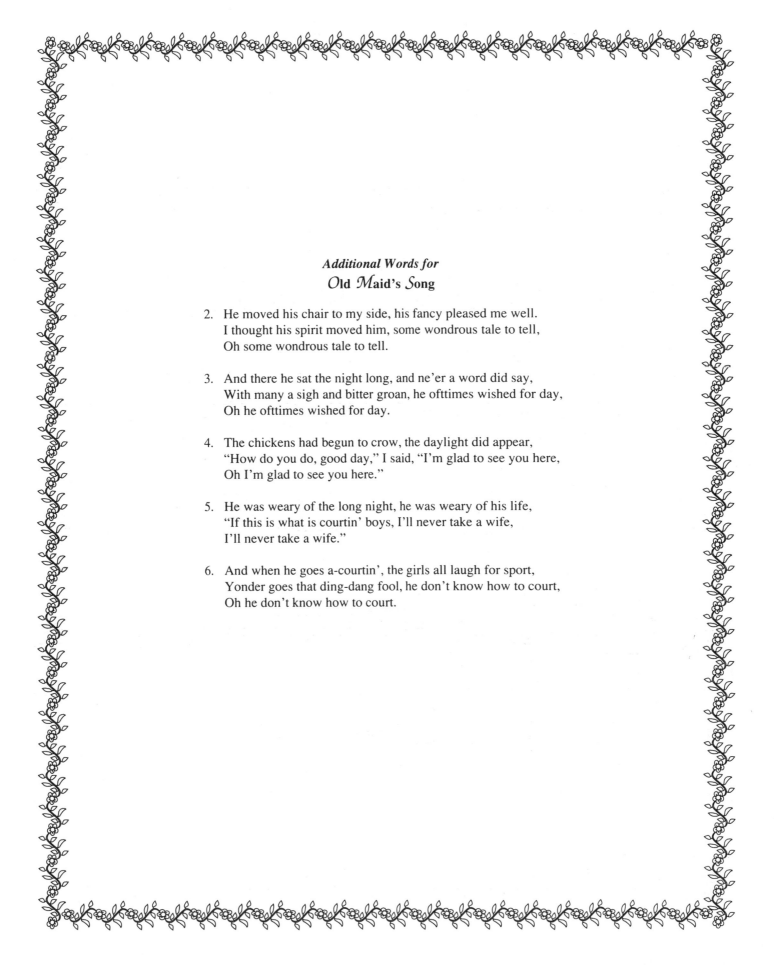

Additional Words for
Old Maid's Song

2. He moved his chair to my side, his fancy pleased me well.
   I thought his spirit moved him, some wondrous tale to tell,
   Oh some wondrous tale to tell.

3. And there he sat the night long, and ne'er a word did say,
   With many a sigh and bitter groan, he ofttimes wished for day,
   Oh he ofttimes wished for day.

4. The chickens had begun to crow, the daylight did appear,
   "How do you do, good day," I said, "I'm glad to see you here,
   Oh I'm glad to see you here."

5. He was weary of the long night, he was weary of his life,
   "If this is what is courtin' boys, I'll never take a wife,
   I'll never take a wife."

6. And when he goes a-courtin', the girls all laugh for sport,
   Yonder goes that ding-dang fool, he don't know how to court,
   Oh he don't know how to court.

Away Out on the Mountain

Text and Air from Nathan Hicks
Banner Elk, NC   July 30, 1933
Collected by Maurice Matteson
Arranged by Richard L. Matteson, Jr.

Slow and Spirited

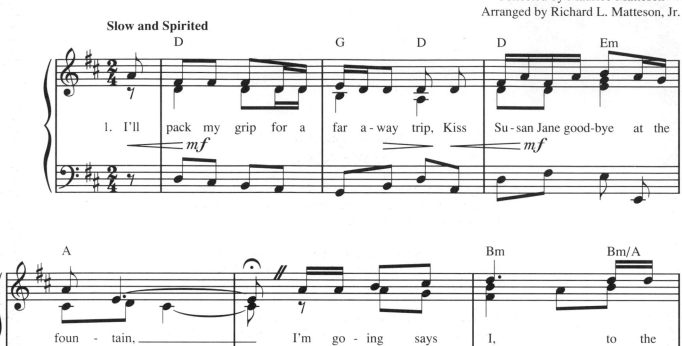

Additional Words for
Away Out on the Mountain

2. Where the wild seed grows and the buffalo lows
    And the squirrels are so many you can't count them,
    There I will make love with the same turtle dove
    Away out on the mountain.

3. When the north winds blow and we're going to have snow,
    And rain and the hail come a-howling,
    I'll send my boats with the buffalo hides
    Away out on the mountain.

4. Where the whippoorwills sing me to sleep at night
    And eagles roost on the rocks of the fountain,
    I'll feast on the meat and the honey so sweet
    Away out on the mountain.

 # Jackaroo

Text and Air from Hubert Brown
Near Asheville, NC   Dec. 29, 1936
Collected by Maurice Matteson
Arranged by Richard L. Matteson, Jr.

1. There was a silk mer - chant, In Lon-don he did dwell. He had an on-ly daugh - ter, The

truth to you I'll tell, the truth to you I'll tell. _____

Additional Words for
Jackaroo

2. She had sweethearts a-plenty
   She courted day and night.
   Till all on Jackie Frazier
   She placed her heart's delight,
   She placed her heart's delight.

3. You may lock me in a dungeon
   It's hard to be confined.
   There's none but Jackie Frazier
   Will ever suit my mind,
   Will ever suit my mind.

4. When her parents saw him coming
   They in an anger flew.
   They gave him forty shillings
   To bear him far away,
   To bear him far away.

5. He sailed all o'er the ocean
   All o'er the deep blue sea.
   So safely he got landed
   In the wars of Germany,
   In the wars of Germany.

6. She went down to the tailor shop
   She dressed in man's array.
   And labored for the captain
   To bear her far away,
   To bear her far away.

7. "Kind sir, your name I'd like to know
   Before on board you go."
   She smiled all in her countenance
   "They call me—'Jackaroo,'
   They call me Jackaroo."

8. She went out to the battlefield
   And viewed it up and down.
   Among the dead and dying
   Her darling boy she found,
   Her darling boy she found.

9. So happily and contented
   They quickly did agree.
   And so they soon got married,
   And why not you and me,
   And why not you and me?

They Stood on the Bridge

Appalachian Source Unknown
Collected by Maurice Matteson
Arranged by Anthony T. Russell

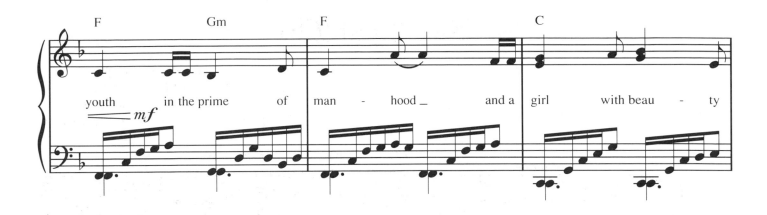

youth   in the prime   of   man - hood _   and a   girl   with beau - ty

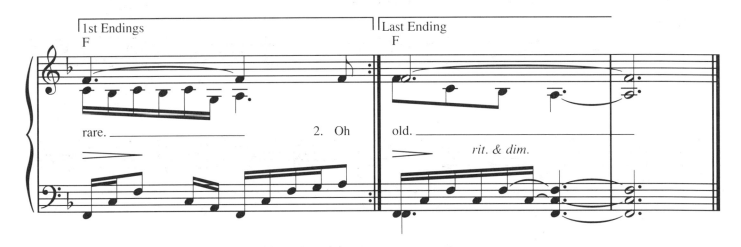

1st Endings

Last Ending

rare. _____

2. Oh

old. _____

rit. & dim.

Additional Words for
*T*hey *S*tood on the *B*ridge

2. "O, I never knew you loved me
   Never knew you'd really care."
   And her proud head bent slowly
   With its wealth of dark brown hair.

3. "O, sir, I was only flirting
   Only playing a part."
   It was only a youth's life blighted
   It was only a broken heart.

4. She looks from her carriage window
   A haunting, beautiful face,
   A proud and stately lady
   All dressed in satin and lace.

5. He goes with the crowd of passers
   Always bitter and cold,
   Only a man grown weary,
   Only a man grown old.

Blue-Eyed Ella

Text and Air from Sarah Pruitt
Cleveland, SC Nov., 1935
Collected by Maurice Matteson
Adapted for piano by Richard L. Matteson, Jr.

Intro

Verse

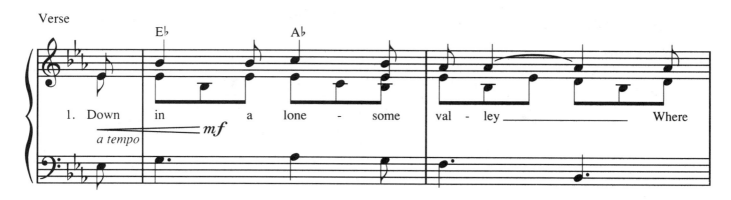

1. Down in a lone - some val - ley _____ Where

vio - lets bloom and fade _____ There's where _____ blue - eyed

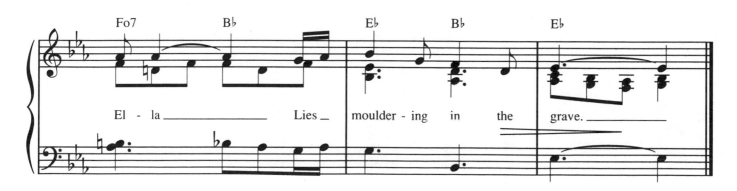

El - la _____ Lies _ moulder - ing in the grave. _____

Additional Words for
Blue-Eyed Ella

2. She died not broken hearted
   Or sickness caused her death,
   It was her jealous lover
   That a dagger pierced her breast.

3. One night the moon was shining
   The stars were shining too,
   'Twas then into her cottage
   Her jealous lover drew.

4. "Come Ella, let's go wandering
   Down in the meadows gay,
   Together we will ponder
   Upon some wedding day."

5. When through a lonesome forest
   He led his love so dear,
   Said she, "It's for you only
   That I have wandered here."

6. "Retrace your steps no, never
   While through this wide world you roam,
   So bid good-bye to parents,
   Loved ones, friends, and home."

7. "Farewell, dear loving parents,
   I may never see you more,
   And long may be my coming
   To the little cottage door."

8. Down on her knees before him,
   She begged him for her life,
   And deep into her bosom
   He plunged the dagger knife.

9. "Now Ella you must forgive me,
   Your parents forgive me too,
   Far in some foreign country
   Where I'll never hear of you."

10. "Yes Edgar, I will forgive you,"
    Was the last deep dying breath,
    "I never have deceived you."
    And closed her eyes in death.

11. When a stranger found her lying
    Cold, lifeless on the ground,
    The flag that waves above her
    Caused a bugle sound.

12. Then Edgar was convicted
    And on the scaffold hung
    For the murder of Blue-eyed Ella
    And the crime that he had done.

Sweet Lillie

Text and Air from Nathan Hicks
Collected by Maurice Matteson
Arranged by Richard L. Matteson, Jr.

Intro
Not Fast

mf

G   Em

G   D7   G

Verse

G   Em

1. I'm going to Georg - ia, I'm going there to roam, I'm
2. (My) foot's in the stir - rup, My reins in ____ my hand, I'm

mf

G   D   G

go - ing to Georg - ia to call it ____ my home. 2. My
court - in' sweet Lil - lie to mar - ry if I can. It's

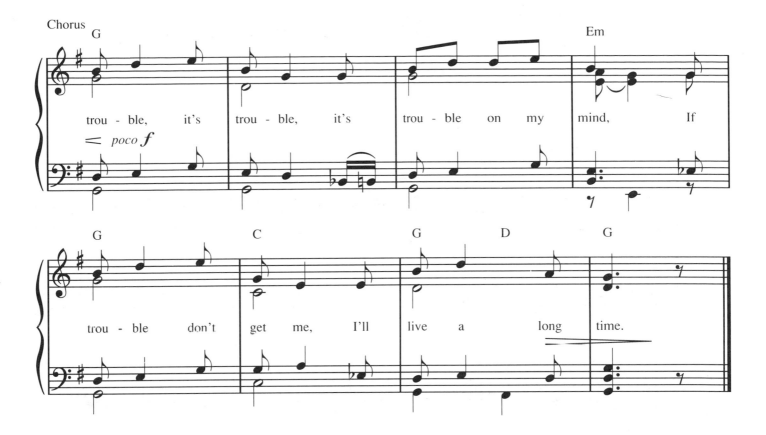

Chorus lyrics (beneath staves):

trou - ble, it's trou - ble, it's trou - ble on my mind, If

trou - ble don't get me, I'll live a long time.

Additional Words for
Sweet Lillie

3. Oh Lillie, sweet Lillie
    Oh, Lillie fare you well,
    I'm sorry to leave you,
    I love you so well.

4. Your parents don't like me,
    Because I am poor;
    They think I'm not worthy,
    To enter your door.

Repeat Chorus

5. Sometimes I drink liquor,
    My money is my own;
    If people don't like me,
    Just leave me alone.

6. Young ladies, young ladies,
    Take warning from me,
    Don't place your affection,
    On a green willow tree.

Repeat Chorus

Once *I* *K*new a *L*ittle *G*irl

Text and Air from Nathan Hicks
Beach Mountain, NC Circa 1933
Collected by Maurice Matteson
Arranged by Anthony Russell

Additional Words for
Once I Knew a Little Girl

2. I took her by her little white hand
   I led her to the door,
   I freely rolled her in my arms,
   And asked her once more
   Oh, and asked her once more.

3. She looked down upon me
   In scorn and disdain,
   "You go off from here and don't you come again,
   And don't you come again,
   Oh, don't you come again."

4. I went off a little while
   To see if she'd complain.
   She wrote me a letter,
   "Oh, please come again,
   Oh, please come again."

5. I wrote her an answer,
   'Twas to let her know,
   That I hadn't forgot the time
   "When you can't come no more
   Oh, when you can't come no more."

6. Come all you people,
   This warning take from me,
   Don't place your affection
   On a green growing tree,
   Oh, on a green growing tree.

7. The tops, they will wither
   The roots will decay;
   The beauty of a young girl
   Will soon fade away
   Oh, will soon fade away.

Star in the East

Mountain Folk Carol
Arranged by Richard L. Matteson, Jr.

Chords: Em (Bm) Em Am (G) D G
dawn on our dark - ness and lend us Thine aid; Star of the East, _ the hor -

Dm G D G
i - zon a - dorn - ing, guide where our in - fant Re - deem - er is laid.

Additional Words for
Star in the East

2. Cold on his cradle the dew-drops are shining,
   Low lies his head with the beasts of the stall;
   Angels adore him in slumber reclining,
   Maker and monarch and Saviour of all.

Chorus: Brightest and best of the sons of the morning,
Dawn on our darkness and lend us Thine aid;
Star of the East, the horizon adorning,
Guide where our infant Redeemer is laid.

3. Say, shall we not yield him in costly devotion,
   Odors of Edom, and off'rings divine,
   Gems of the mountain and pearls of the ocean,
   Myrrh from the forest, and gold from the mine? *(Chorus)*

4. Vainly we offer each ample oblation,
   Vainly with gifts would his favor secure;
   Richer by far is the heart's adoration,
   Dearer to God are the prayers of the poor. *(Chorus)*

5. Low at his feet we in humble prostration,
   Lose all our sorrow and trouble and strife;
   There we receive his divine consolation,
   Flowing afresh from the fountain of life. *(Chorus)*

6. He is our friend in the midst of temptation,
   Faithful supporter, whose love cannot fail;
   Rock of our refuge, and hope of salvation,
   Light to direct us through death's gloomy vale. *(Chorus)*

7. Star of the morning, thy brightness, declining,
   Shortly must fade when the sun doth arise;
   Beaming refulgent, his glory eternal
   Shines on the children of love in the skies. *(Chorus)*

I Gave My Love a Cherry

(Riddle Song)

Text and Air from Mollye Wilcox
Berea, KY Circa 1934
Collected by Maurice Matteson
Arranged by Richard L. Matteson, Jr.

Additional Words for

I Gave My Love a Cherry

2. How can there be a cherry that has no stone?
   How can there be a chicken that has no bone?
   How can there be a ring that has no end?
   How can there be a baby with no cryin'?

3. A cherry when it's bloomin', it has no stone,
   A chicken when it's pippin', it has no bone,
   A ring when it's rolling, it has no end,
   A baby when it's sleeping has no cryin'.

Sourwood Mountain

Text and Air from Zeb Dixon
Black Mountain, NC
Collected by Maurice Matteson
Arranged for piano by Anthony T. Russell

Intro

Fast, Lively

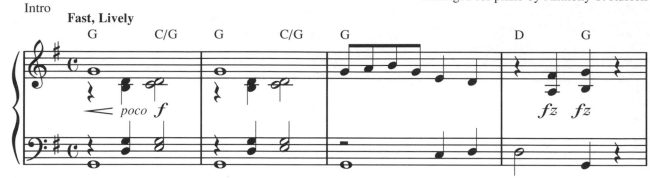

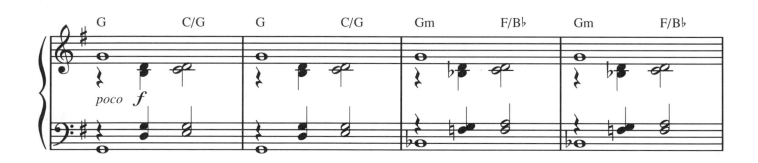

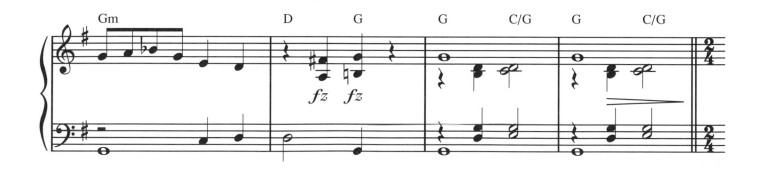

Verse

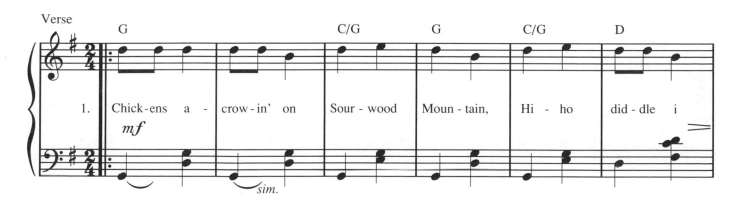

1. Chick-ens a - crow-in' on Sour-wood Moun-tain, Hi - ho did-dle i

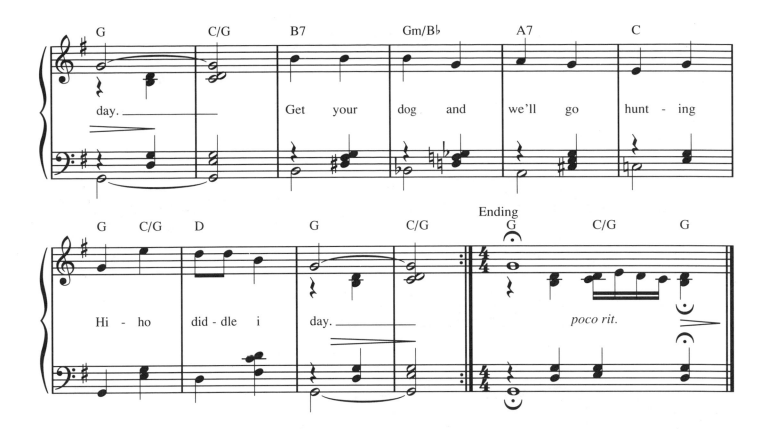

Additional Words for
Sourwood Mountain

2. I gotta girl in the head of the hollow,
   Hi ho diddle i day.
   She won't come and I won't call her,
   Hi ho diddle i day.

3. She sits up there with ole Si Hall,
   Hi ho diddle i day.
   Me and Jim can't go a-tall,
   Hi ho diddle i day.

4. One of these days and it won't be long,
   Hi ho diddle i day.
   I'll get that girl and home I'll be gone,
   Hi ho diddle i day.

Sinful to Flirt

Text and Air from the singing of Nathan Hicks
Beach Mountain, NC
Collected by Maurice Matteson
Arranged by Richard L. Matteson, Jr.

1. They say it is sin - ful to flirt, That my heart is ___ hard like a stone. They say to treat him ___ kind, Or else let the poor boy a - lone.

Additional Words for
Sinful to Flirt

2. They say he is only a boy,
   Yet I am sure he is older than me,
   But if they would leave us alone
   I am sure we would happier be.

3. I remember last night when he said
   That he loved me far better than life.
   He called me his darling, his own,
   And asked me to be his wife.

4. "Willie," I said with a smile,
   "I am sure I will have to say, no,"
   Then he took a white rose from my hair
   And said, "Good-bye, I must go."

5. Next morning poor Willie was dead
   He was drowned in the pond by the mill
   In the water so still, pure, and clear
   That flows from the brink of the hill.

6. His eyes forever were closed
   Dark was his bright golden hair
   And close to his pale lips he held the white rose
   That he took from my hair.

7. O Willie, my darling, come back,
   I will ever be faithful and true
   O Willie, my darling, come back,
   I will ever be faithful and true.

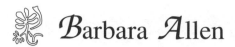

Barbara Allen

Text and Air from the singing of Cleo Franklyn
Smyth Co., VA   July 14, 1934
Collected by Maurice Matteson
Arranged by Cindy E. Long

1. Late in the sea - son of the year. The yel-low leaves are fall - ing _ Sweet Wil-liam he _ was tak - en sick for the love of Bar - ba-ra Al - len _ 2. He sent his mes - sen-ger to the town, The town where she was dwell-ing, _ Rise you up to your

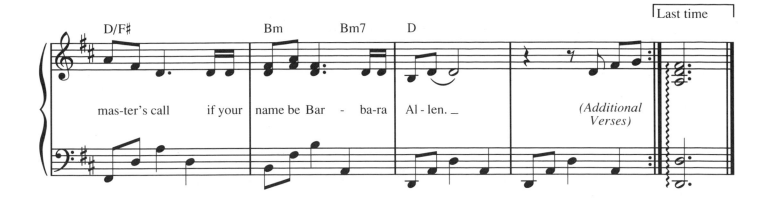

master's call   if your | name be Bar - ba-ra | Al - len. _   *(Additional Verses)*

Additional Words for
Barbara Allen

3. So slowly, slowly she got up,
   And slowly she went unto him.
   Pulled the curtains from around his head,
   Said, "Young man I think you're dying."

4. "Oh yes I'm low, I'm low indeed,
   And death is in my dwelling.
   Never better will I ever be,
   Until I get Barbara Allen."

5. "Oh don't you remember in yonder town,
   The town where you were dwelling?
   You treated ladies all around,
   And slighted Barbara Allen."

6. "Oh yes I remember in yonder town,
   The town where I was dwelling;
   I treated ladies all around,
   And slighted Barbara Allen."

7. He turned his pale face to the wall
   His back he turned to her.
   He said to the ladies standing 'round,
   "Be kind to Barbara Allen."

8. She had not got three miles from town
   She heard the death bell tolling.
   She thought she heard her own heart beat,
   Stop—stop—Barbara Allen.

9. She looked to the East and to the West
   She saw the corpse a-coming.
   "Do lie down this very young man,
   While I do gaze upon him."

10. The more she looked the more she wept
    Till she burst out a-crying;
    "Oh take from me this very young man,
    I think that I am dying."

11. They took him to the new church yard,
    And that is where they laid him.
    They buried his lover by his side,
    Her name—was Barbara Allen.

12. Out of his grave there sprang a rose,
    And out of hers a briar;
    They grew and tied a true lover's knot,
    The rose around the briar.

The Weeping Lady

Text and Air from Mollye Wilcox
Berea, KY   Aug. 20, 1935
Collected and Arranged by Maurice Matteson

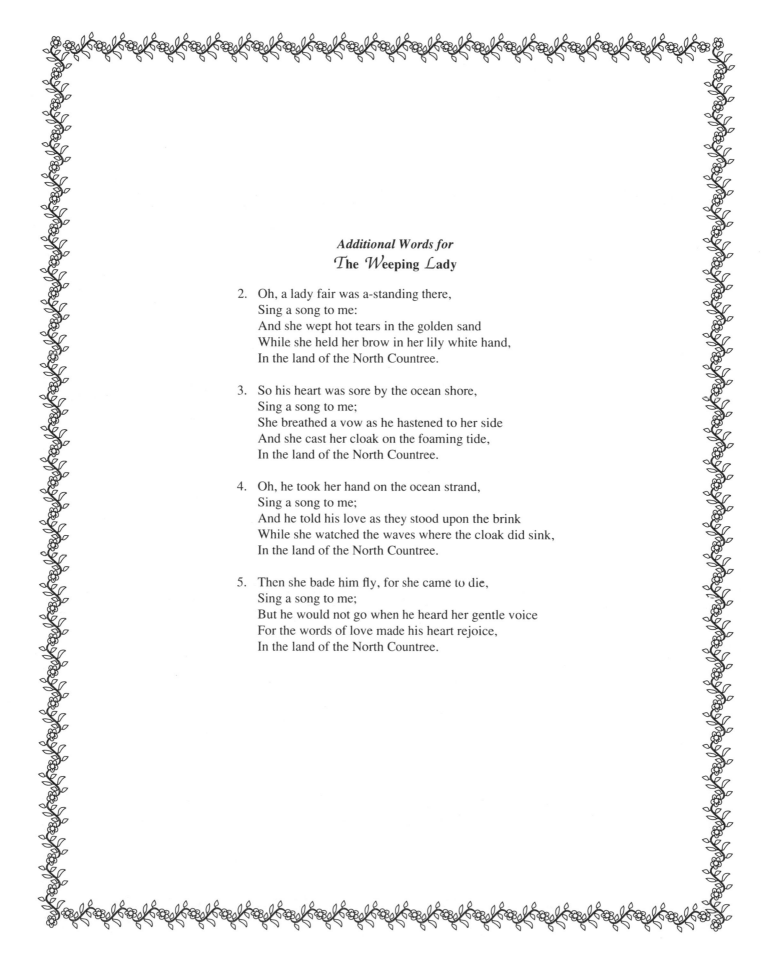

Additional Words for
The Weeping Lady

2. Oh, a lady fair was a-standing there,
   Sing a song to me:
   And she wept hot tears in the golden sand
   While she held her brow in her lily white hand,
   In the land of the North Countree.

3. So his heart was sore by the ocean shore,
   Sing a song to me;
   She breathed a vow as he hastened to her side
   And she cast her cloak on the foaming tide,
   In the land of the North Countree.

4. Oh, he took her hand on the ocean strand,
   Sing a song to me;
   And he told his love as they stood upon the brink
   While she watched the waves where the cloak did sink,
   In the land of the North Countree.

5. Then she bade him fly, for she came to die,
   Sing a song to me;
   But he would not go when he heard her gentle voice
   For the words of love made his heart rejoice,
   In the land of the North Countree.

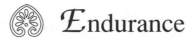

Endurance

Text and Air from the singing of Nathan Hicks
Sugar Grove, NC
Collected by Maurice Matteson
Arranged by Richard L. Matteson, Jr.

Intro
Slowly with Pathos

Verse

1. The day I left my moth-er's house was the

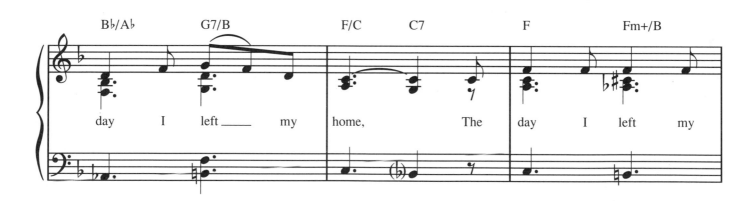

day I left ____ my home, The day I left my

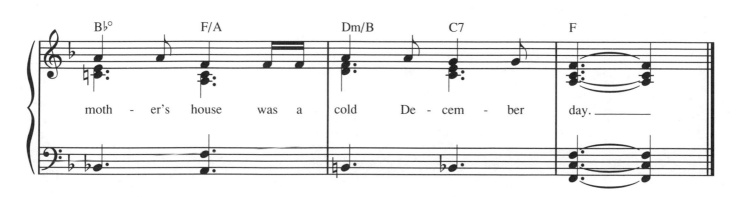

moth-er's house was a cold De-cem-ber day. ____

Additional Words for
Endurance

2. The sky was dark and cloudy,
   To me it looked like rain.
   I wished for a friend in the whole wide world,
   Just one who knew my name.

3. I walked out to the road side
   To see the passers by,
   And there I saw the woman I loved,
   She had rode for many a mile.

4. "O, you have brought me silver
   Or you have brought me gold,
   Have you brought me nothing
   to keep me from the gallow's pole?"

It Rained

Text and Air from the singing of Mrs. J.E. Shell
Banner Elk, NC   July 15, 1933
Collected by Maurice Matteson
Arranged for piano by Richard and Ann Matteson

Intro **With Movement**

Verse

1. It rained it rained, it rained it rained, it rained all o - ver the

town. Two lit-tle boys came out to play, For to toss their balls and

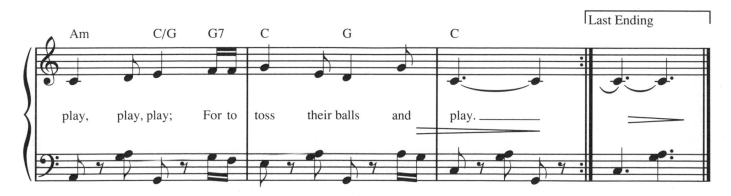

play, play, play; For to toss their balls and play.

Additional Words for
It Rained

2. At first they tossed it too high
   And then they tossed it too low,
   And then they tossed it in a vacant yard
   Where no one was allowed to go, go, go,
   Where no one was allowed to go.

3. A lady came out all dressed in silk,
   All dressed in silk so fine,
   "Come in, come in, my little boy,
   And you shall have your ball, ball, ball,
   And you shall have your ball."

4. At first she showed him a fine gold watch,
   And then she showed him a chain,
   And then she showed him a diamond ring,
   Which fit his little hand so neat, neat, neat,
   Which fit his hand so neat.

5. She pinned a napkin around his head;
   She pinned it with a pin;
   And in her hand was a carving knife;
   She stabbed his little heart in, in, in,
   She stabbed his little heart in.

6. "Oh, spare my life, Oh, spare my life,
   Oh, spare my life," he cried;
   "If ever I grow up to be a man,
   I'll do some labor for you, you, you,
   I'll do some labor for you."

7. "Please place the Testament at my head,
   And the Bible at my feet;
   If mother and father should call for me
   Please tell them that I'm a-sleep, sleep, sleep,
   Please tell them that I'm asleep."

8. "Please place the Testament at my feet
   And the Bible at my head;
   If any of my friends should call for me,
   Please tell them that I'm dead, dead, dead,
   Please tell them that I'm dead."

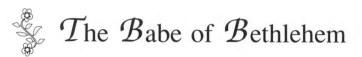

The Babe of Bethlehem

Shape Note Carol
Arranged by Richard L. Matteson, Jr.

Moderately M.M. ♩ = 80

1. Ye na - tions all, ___ on ye I call, Come hear this dec - la - ra - tion, And don't re - fuse __ this glo - rious news of Je - sus and __ sal - va - tion. To roy - al __ Jews came first the __ news of Christ, the great __ Mes - si - ah. As 'twas fore - told __ by proph - ets old, I - sai - ah, Je - re - mi - ah.

Additional Words for
The Babe of Bethlehem

2. His parents poor in earthly store
   To entertain the stranger
   They found no bed to lay His head,
   But in the ox's manger:
   No royal things, as used by kings,
   Were seen by those that found Him,
   But in the hay the stranger lay,
   With swaddling bands around Him.

3. On the same night a glorious light
   To the shepherds there appeared
   Bright angels came in shining flame,
   They saw and greatly feared.
   The angels said, "Be not afraid,
   Although we much alarm you,
   We do appear good news to bear,
   As now we will inform you.

4. "The city's name is Bethlehem,
   In which God hath appointed,
   This glorious morn a Savior's born,
   For Him God hath anointed.
   By this you'll know, if you will go,
   To see this little stranger,
   His lovely charms in Mary's arms,
   Both lying in a manger."

5. When this was said, straightway was made
   A glorious sound from heaven,
   Each flaming tongue an anthem sung,
   "To men a Savior's given,
   In Jesus's name, the glorious theme
   We elevate our voices,
   At Jesus' birth be peace on earth,
   Meanwhile all heaven rejoices."

6. Then with delight they took their flight,
   And wing'd their way to glory,
   The shepherds gazed and were amazed,
   To hear the pleasing story;
   To Bethlehem they quickly came,
   The glorious news to carry,
   And in the stall they found them all,
   Joseph, the Babe, and Mary.

7. The shepherds then return'd again
   To their own habitation
   With joy of heart they did depart,
   Now they have found salvation.
   Glory, they cry, to God on high,
   Who sent His Son to save us
   This glorious morn the Savior's born,
   His name it is Christ Jesus.

One Morning in May

Singer Unknown
Pine Mountain, KY   Aug. 18, 1935
Collected by Maurice Matteson
Arranged by Richard L. Matteson, Jr.

Additional Words for
One Morning in May

2. "Good morning, good morning, good morning to you
   Oh where are you going my pretty lady?"
   "Oh I'm going walking beside of the sea
   To see waters gliding, hear nightingales sing."

3. They had not been standing but one hour or two
   When out of his knapsack a fiddle he drew.
   The tune that he played made the valleys ring
   "Listen," said the lady, "How the nightingales sing."

4. "Oh no, pretty lady, 'tis time to give o'er."
   "Oh no, pretty soldier, please play one tune more.
   I'd rather hear you fiddle or touch of one string,
   Than to see waters gliding or the nightingale sing."

5. "Oh say pretty soldier will you marry me?"
   "Oh no pretty lady that never can be:
   I've a wife in London, and children you see
   Two wives in the army's too many for me."

6. "I'll go back to London and stay there a year
   And often I'll think of you, my little dear:
   And when I return it will be in the spring
   To see waters gliding and hear nightingales sing."

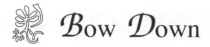

Bow Down

Text and Air from Hubert Brown
Near Ashville, NC   Dec. 29, 1936
Collected by Maurice Matteson
Arranged by Richard L. Matteson, Jr.

1. There was an old man in the North Coun - tree   Bow down.

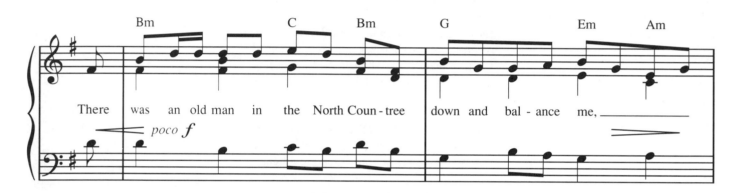

There was an old man in the North Coun - tree   down and bal - ance me, _____

He had daugh-ters one, two, three. I'll be   true to you my love if you're true to   me. _____

Additional Words for
Bow Down

2. He bought the youngest a silken hat
   Bow down.
   He bought the youngest a silken hat
   Bow down and balance me.
   His eldest daughter she couldn't stand that.
   I'll be true to you my love, if you'll be true to me.

3. They walked down by the water's brim
   Bow down.
   They walked down by the water's brim
   Bow down and balance me.
   His eldest pushed the youngest in.
   I'll be true to you my love, if you'll be true to me.

4. She floated down to the miller's dam
   Bow down.
   She floated down to the miller's dam
   Bow down and balance me.
   The miller pushed her to dry ground.
   I'll be true to you my love, if you'll be true to me.

5. From her hand he took five rings
   Bow down.
   From her hand he took five rings
   Bow down and balance me.
   Then he pushed her in again.
   I'll be true to you my love, if you'll be true to me.

6. They hung the miller on the gallows high
   Bow down.
   They hung the miller on the gallows high
   Bow down and balance me.
   The eldest daughter, she hung near by.
   I'll be true to you my love, if you'll be true to me.

Willow Garden

Appalachian Source Unknown
Collected by Maurice Matteson
Arranged by Anthony T. Russell and Richard L. Matteson, Jr.

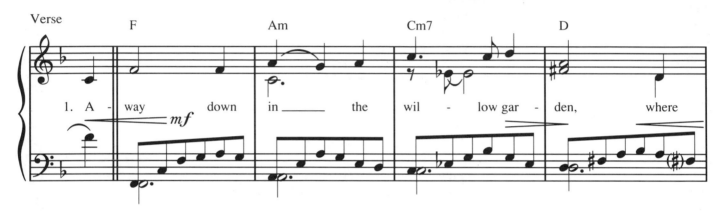

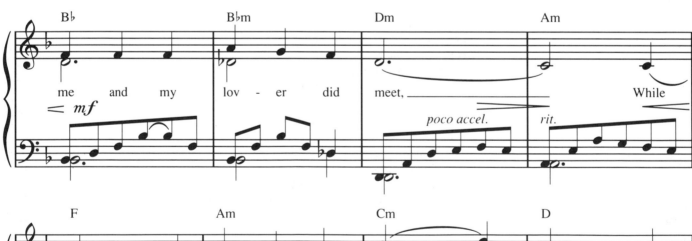

lov - er ____ dropped off to sleep.

Last Ending

mf

poco rit. & dim.

Additional Words for
Willow Garden

2. I had a bottle of Burglar's wine,
   Which my true love did not know.
   And there I poisoned my own true love,
   Down under the banks below.

3. I threw my sovereign through her,
   Which would her blood deny.
   I threw her in the river,
   Which was an awful sight.

4. I threw her in the river,
   Which was a sight to see.
   My name is Panama Reidio
   Who murdered Rose Carnalee.

5. My father always taught me,
   That money would set me free.
   If I would murder this fair young girl,
   Whose name was Rose Carnalee.

6. But now he sits in his cottage door,
   And wipes his weeping eyes.
   And looks upon his only son,
   Who must hang on the gallows high.

7. Beneath the sun, my race is run,
   Lord, hell is a-waiting me.
   My name is Panama Reidio,
   Who murdered Rose Carnalee.

Froggie Went a-Courtin'

Appalachian Source Unknown
Collected by Maurice Matteson
Arranged by Maurice Matteson

Additional Words for
Froggie Went a-Courtin'

2. He rode right up to Miss Mousie's door, he did,
   He rode right up to Miss Mousie's door,
   He hit it hard and made it roar.
       Un-huh, un-huh.

3. He took Miss Mousie on his knee, he did,
   He took Miss Mousie on his knee,
   He said, "Miss Mousie will you marry me?"
       Un-huh, un-huh.

4. She said, "I can not answer that," she did,
   She said, "I can not answer that,
   Until I ask Old Uncle Rat."
       Un-huh, un-huh.

5. Old Uncle Rat gave his consent, he did,
   Old Uncle Rat gave his consent,
   And they were married quite content.
       Un-huh, un-huh.

The Sheffield Apprentice

Text and Air from Mrs. Padgett
Black Mountain, NC   July 18, 1934
Collected by Maurice Matteson
Arranged by Ann and Richard L. Matteson, Jr.

I was bound a pren-tice and then my joys were fled.

mf

Additional Words for
The Sheffield Apprentice

3. I did not like my master, he did not treat me well;
   I formed a resolution, not long with him to dwell.

4. Against my parents' wishes from home I ran away.
   And then away to London but cursed be that day.

5. A rich and royal lady from Holland, she was there.
   She offered me great wages to servant for one year.

6. With wages and persuasions with her I did agree.
   I went and lived in Holland, but that's what ruined me.

7. I had not been in Holland, passed months
        but two or three,
   Until my honored lady, grew very fond of me.

8. She offered me her silver, her houses and her lands;
   If I would consent to marry her and be at her command.

9. Says: "No, my dear young lady, I cannot wed you both
   For I have lately promised, and swore a solemn oath.

10. "To marry none but Polly, the pretty chamber maid.
    Excuse my dear mistress, she has my heart beleagued.

11. She flew in an angry passion, away from me she ran,
    She swore that she would have revenge
            before that deed was done.

12. By her being objected and could not be my wife;
    She seemed to seek a project to take away my life.

13. One bright and beautiful morning, all in the month of May.
    The flowers they were blooming, delightfully and gay.

14. Her gold ring from her finger, as I was passing by;
    She slipped into my pocket; which caused me to die.

15. She swore that I had robbed her, and quickly I was brought
    Before a brave old justice to answer for my fault.

16. A long time I pled innocent; but it was no revail;
    She swore so hard against me that I was sent to jail.

17. Come all who stand around me my wretched face to see
    who glory in my downfall, but I pray you pity me.

18. Believe that I'm quite innocent; I'll bid this world adieu.
    So fare you well my Polly, I die for loving you.

The Fox

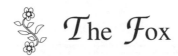

Text and Air from Grace Alder, Tenn.
Collected by Maurice Matteson
Arranged by Ann Matteson

Additional Words for
The Fox

2. He came at last to the farmer's yard,
   Where the ducks and chickens were plenty.
   "Oh, one of you will grease my beard,
   I'll take you to my den-e-o,
   I'll take you to my den-e-o."

3. He grabbed an old black duck by the neck,
   And he threw her across his shoulder.
   The old black duck said, "Quack! Quack!"
   And its long legs hung down-e-o,
   And its long legs hung down-e-o.

4. Old Granny Slipper Slopper jumped out of bed,
   And out the window poked her grey head.
   "John, John, the black duck's gone,
   With the fox straight to his den-e-o,
   With the fox straight to his den-e-o."

5. Old Johnny Slipper Slopper jumped out of bed,
   He fell against the table and he bumped his head.
   He fell over the cradle and thought he was dead,
   And the fox got to his den-e-o,
   And the fox got to his den-e-o.

6. Old Slipper Slopper ran to the top of the hill,
   And he blew his horn so loud and shrill.
   But the fox got the best of the music still,
   Safe home inside his den-e-o,
   Safe home inside his den-e-o.

The Brown Girl

Text and Air from Louisa Hubbard
Brock, KY   Aug. 16, 1933
Collected by Maurice Matteson
Arranged by Richard L. Matteson, Jr.

With Movement

1. Come rid - dle, come rid - dle me, dear moth - er. Come
rid - dle me one that I should have Fair El - len -
der _____ for my bride; Or bring the Brown Girl
home, home; Or bring the Brown Girl home.

2. "The Brown Girl she has house and land
   Fair Ellender she has none;
   I'll give your choice my own blessing
   To bring the Brown Girl home, home,
   To bring the Brown Girl home."

3. He dressed, he dressed himself in brown
   His armlets all in red.
   And every town he rode around
   They took him to be some Lord, Lord,
   They took him to be some Lord.

4. He rode, he rode to Fair Ellender's gate
   He jingled on the ring.
   There were none so ready as Fair Ellender herself
   To rise and let him come in, in
   To rise and let him come in.

5. "What news, what news, what news?" said she,
   "What news have you brought to me?"
   "I've come to ask you to my own wedding,
   Tomorrow night shall be, be
   Tomorrow night shall be.

6. "Bad news, bad news, bad news," said she;
   "Bad news you have brought to me.
   I thought that I was your bride myself
   While you the bridegroom be, be
   While you the bridegroom be."

7. "Come riddle, come riddle me, dear mother
   Come riddle me as one.
   That I should go to Lord Thomas's wedding
   Or stay and tarry at home, home
   Or stay and tarry at home."

8. "Oh daughter, oh daughter, you friends you know
   And you have foes as well.
   I'll give you choice of my blessing
   To stay and tarry at home, home
   To stay and tarry at home."

9. She dressed, she dressed herself in red
   Her armlets all in green.
   And every town she rode around
   They took her to be some queen, queen
   They took her to be some queen.

10. She rode, she rode Lord Thomas's gate
    She jingled on the ring.
    There was none so ready as Lord Thomas himself
    To rise and let her come in, in
    To rise and let her come in.

11. He took her by the lily-white hand
    He led her in a hall.
    He sat her down at the head of the table
    Amongst the quality all, all
    Amongst the quality all.

12. "Lord Thomas Lord Thomas is this your bride?
    I'd say she's very brown.
    When you might have had the fairest one
    That ever the sun shone on, on
    That ever the sun shone on."

13. The Brown Girl she had a little penknife
    And it was both keen and sharp.
    Betwixt her long rib and her short
    She pressed it against her heart, her heart
    She pressed it against her heart.

14. "Lord Thomas, Lord Thomas are you blind
    Or can you scarcely see?
    The only blood from my heart
    Come trickling to my knee, knee
    Come trickling to my knee."

15. He took the Brown Girl by her hand
    He led her from the hall.
    He drew a sword, cut off her head
    And kicked it against the wall, wall
    And kicked it against the wall.

16. He put the sword against the floor
    The point against his breast.
    Saying, "Here is the end of three love lives
    God send their souls to rest, rest
    God send their souls to rest."

17. "Go dig my grave both wide and deep
    And paint my coffin black.
    And bury Fair Ellender in my arms,
    The Brown Girl at my back, back
    The Brown Girl at my back."

18. "Go dig my grave both deep and wide
    On my breast place a turtle dove.
    And this will show all the world
    That we died for love, love
    That we died for love."

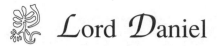
Lord Daniel

From the singing of Miss Vivian Pike
Garrett Co., MD   1940
Collected and Arranged by Maurice Matteson
Adapted for piano by Richard L. Matteson, Jr.

Additional Words for
*L*ord *D*aniel

2. Little Massie gazed at the next came down—
   She was looking awfully nice.
   He knew by the ring that she wore on her hand
   That she was Lord Daniel's wife—
   That she was Lord Daniel's wife.

3. Little Willie was standing right close by
   And heard every word that was said.
   Said, "If I live till tomorrow morn
   Lord Daniel will hear of this,
   Lord Daniel will hear of this."

4. Little Willie had three miles to go
   And half of this he ran;
   And he ran till he came to broken bridge.
   He fell on his breast and swam;
   Lord, he fell on his breast and swam!

5. He swam and swam till he came grass green;
   He got on his feet and ran.
   He ran till he came Lord Daniel's house
   He rattled them bells and rang,
   Lord, he rattled them bells and rang!

6. Lord Daniel said: "Why are you here?
   And why did you come?"
   "Your wife's at home with another man,
   And both of their hearts are one—
   Lord, both of their hearts are one!

7. Lord Daniel said: "Have you told me a lie
   Which I have taken it to be.
   I'll take you to the Pialet Knob,
   I'll hang you to a tree,
   Lord, I'll hang you to a tree!"

8. Lord Daniel walked right straight home
   And there he took a peep.
   He found his belovèd wife
   In Massie's arms asleep;
   Lord, in Massie's arms asleep!

9. Lord Daniel walked right straight in,
   And he was looking awful.
   Says, "You can fight any way you please
   But I'm going to fight to kill,
   Lord, I'm going to fight to kill!"

10. Little Massie said, "Lord, I will, Sir.
    Please spare me my life
    That you have two noble swords
    And I have got no knife,
    Lord, I have got no knife!"

11. "Yes, I have two noble swords,
    They cost me deep in my purse.
    I'll give to you the very best one.
    I'm going to take the worst,
    Lord, I'm going to take the worst!"

12. Little Massie struck the very first lick
    With his awful sword.
    Lord Daniel struck the very next lick,
    Killed Little Massie on the floor,
    Killed Little Massie on the floor!

13. He took her by her lily-white hand,
    He pulled her on his knee.
    Says, "Which of the two do you love the best?
    Little Massie's gold or me?
    Little Massie's gold or me?"

14. "Very well, I love your rosy red cheeks,
    Very well, I love your chin,
    But I would not give Little Massie's gold
    For you and all your kin,
    For you and all your kin!"

15. He took her by her lily-white hand
    And he led her in the hall.
    He placed a pistol to her heart
    Let her have a special ball,
    Let her have a special ball.

16. Go dig my grave on yonder hill.
    Go dig it wide and deep!
    And bury Little Massie in my arms,
    Lord Daniel at my feet,
    Lord Daniel at my feet.

Kind Miss, I've Come a-Courtin'

Text and Air from Cleo Franklyn
Smyth Co., VA   July 14, 1934
Collected by Maurice Matteson
Arranged by Richard L. Matteson, Jr.

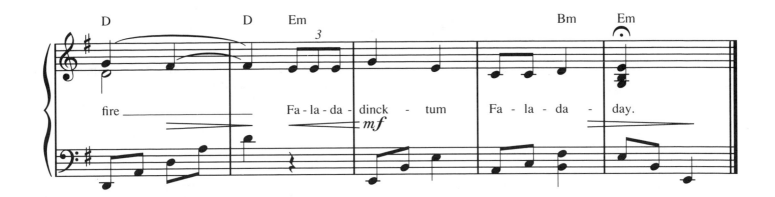

Additional Words for

𝒦ind 𝓜iss, 𝐼've 𝒞ome a-𝒞ourtin'

2. I have a ring worth many a shilling. Oh, dear me.
   And you may wear it if you're willing. Oh, dear me.

   Chorus: Well if that is your intention,
   Fa-la-da-dincktum, fa-la-da-day.
   You can sit and court the fire,
   Fa-la-da-dincktum, fa-la-da-day.

3. Don't want your ring, don't want your money. Oh, dear me.
   Don't want any man to call me honey. Oh, dear me. *(Repeat Chorus)*

4. She called her dogs and set them on me. Oh, dear me.
   Oh my, oh my, how they run me. Oh, dear me. *(Repeat Chorus)*

5. You'd better run for I don't like you. Oh, dear me.
   If they catch you they will bite you. Oh, dear me. *(Repeat Chorus)*

Four Nights

From the singing of Mrs. Mollie Hampton,
Elk Park, NC   Aug. 7, 1933
Collected by Maurice Matteson
Arranged for piano by
Anthony T. Russell and Richard L. Matteson, Jr.

Intro

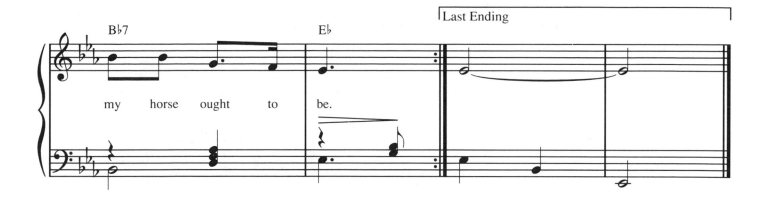

Additional Words for
Four Nights

2. Come here, little wifie,
   Explain yourself to me.
   Why is this horse in the stable
   Where my horse ought to be?

3. You blame fool, you crazy fool,
   Can't you never see?
   It's only a milk-cow
   My mammy give to me.

4. I've been living in this wide world
   Forty years or more;
   I never seen a milk-cow
   With a saddle on before.

5. The second night when I come home,
   As drunk as I could be,
   I saw a coat hanging on the rack
   Where my coat ought to be.

6. Come here, little wifie,
   Explain yourself to me.
   Why is this coat hanging on the rack
   Where my coat ought to be?

7. You blame fool, you crazy fool,
   Can't you never see?
   It's only a cover-lid
   My mammy give to me.

8. I've been living in this wide world
   Forty years or more;
   I never seen a cover-lid
   With buttons on before.

9. The third night when I come home,
   As drunk as I could be,
   I saw boots standing in the corner
   Where my boots ought to be.

10. Come here, little wifie,
    Explain yourself to me.
    Why are these boots standing in the corner
    Where my boots ought to be?

11. You blame fool, you crazy fool,
    Can't you never see?
    It's only a cream jar
    My mammy give to me.

12. I've been living in this wide world
    Forty years or more;
    I never seen a cream jar
    With booties on before.

13. The fourth night when I come home,
    As drunk as I could be,
    I saw a head lying on the bed
    Where my head ought to be.

14. Come here, little wifie,
    Explain yourself to me.
    Why is this head lying on the bed
    Where my head ought to be?

15. You blame fool, you crazy fool,
    Can't you never see:
    It's only a cabbage head
    My mammy give to me.

16. I've been living in this wide world
    Forty years or more;
    I never seen a cabbage head
    With a moustache on before.

Sweet Willie

Text and Air from Mrs. Lloyd Bragg
Elk Park, NC   Aug. 7, 1933
Arranged by Anthony T. Russell and Richard L. Matteson, Jr.

Intro
Slow

Verse

1. He rode up to the old man's gate, And

bold - ly _____ he did say, "You

keep your young - est daugh - ter at home, _ but the

old - est one I will take a - way.

mf

mf

Additional Words for
Sweet Willie

2. He got on his milk-white steed
   And she on her dapple gray;
   He swung his bugle-horn around his neck
   And they went riding away.

3. They had not gone more than a mile and a half
   Until they both looked back.
   They saw her father and seven of her brothers
   Come trippling over the slack.

4. "Crawl right down," Sweet Willie cried,
   "And hold my milk-white steed
   Till I fight your father and seven of your brothers,
   Or die in my own life's blood."

5. She got right down without one word,
   And helt the milk-white steed
   Till she saw her father and seven of her brothers
   Go dying in their own hearts' blood.

6. "Oh, slack your hand, Sweet Willie," she cried,
   "Your wounds are deep and sore.
   Oh, slack your hand, Sweet Willie," she cried,
   "For father I can have no more."

7. "If you don't like what I have done,
   You can love some other one;
   I wish you away in your mother's chamberee,
   And me in some house or room."

8. They rode on to his father's gate
   And tapped against the ring.
   "O father, O mother, asleep or awake,
   Arise and let me in."

9. Sweet Willie died like it was today;
   Fair Ellen died tomorrow.
   Sweet Willie died of the wounds that he received;
   Fair Ellen she died of sorrow.

Folk Song Notes

The Cuckoo   One of the most beautiful minor song melodies found in the Appalachians, this melody is from Maurice Matteson's unpublished manuscript, *Three Kentucky Folk Songs for Soprano, Alto and Tenor.* Dr. Matteson collected the text and air from the singing of Mrs. Joseph A. Gaines, Glasgow, Kentucky on August 30, 1936. The arrangement for piano solo is by Ann S. Matteson and Richard L. Matteson, Jr.

A similar version is found in Cecil Sharp's *Eighty English Folk Songs from the Southern Appalachians*, #38, p. 61. "The Cuckoo" has many related folk songs including "A-Walkin' and A-Talkin'" and "The Turtle Dove" and compares with "The Wagoner's Lad."

The Old Shoemaker   Also from Maurice Matteson's unpublished *Three Kentucky Folk Songs for Soprano, Alto and Tenor*, the text and air is from Mrs. Joseph Gaines, Glasgow, Kentucky on August 30, 1936. The piano arrangement is by Ann S. Matteson and Richard L. Matteson, Jr.

Additional verses are from Sharp's EFSSA p. 285:

> Go hand me down my pegging awl
> I stuck it right up yonder,
> Go hand me down my sewing awl
> To peg and sew my leather
>
> I have lost my shoemaker's wax
> And where do you think I'll find it?
> O ain't that enough to break my heart.
> O right here, Kate, I've found it.

(A Frail) Wildwood Flower   The tune first appeared in Maurice Matteson's *Beech Mountain Ballads* published in 1936 by G. Schirmer, which may have been the first published version of the now popular tune. The text and air are taken from the singing of Miss Edith Robbins, Banner Elk, NC, August 5, 1933. The piano arrangement is by Maurice Matteson.

The Rosewood Casket   Also appeared in Maurice Matteson's *Beech Mountain Ballads*. The text is from Nathan Hicks and the air is from Edward Tufts, Banner Elk, NC, July 25, 1933. The tune is arranged for piano solo by Cindy Long.

Hush, My Babe   The beautiful Christmas carol appears with a different arrangement in Richard Matteson's *An Appalachian Christmas*, published by Mel Bay in 1993. The melody of this cradle hymn is also found as the shape-note hymn, *Restoration*. The words are from the 14 stanza poem by Isaac Watts. A great version of this tune is sung by Doc Watson of Deep Gap, NC.

Old Maid's Song   This charming melody and humorous lyric in Maurice Matteson's unpublished manuscript collection is from Mollye Willcox, Berea, Kentucky, August 17, 1933. The piano solo has been arranged by Rebekah Fishel and Richard L. Matteson, Jr.

Away Out on the Mountain   One of the tunes featured in Maurice Matteson's article on song collecting *Wanted! Mountain Music* p. 9–p. 13 (see "Away Out on the Mountain"). This folk song is one of the first Maurice Matteson collected in the Beech Mountain area from Nathan Hicks, Banner Elk, NC on July 30, 1933. The piano arrangement is by Richard L. Matteson, Jr.

Jackaroo   One of the fine English ballads from Maurice Matteson's unpublished collection, this text and minor air are from the singing of Hubert Brown near Asheville, NC, December 29, 1936. The arrangement is by Richard L. Matteson, Jr.

"Jackaroo" is a version of the English ballad, "The Silk Merchant's Daughter," appearing in Sharp's EFSSA as No. 54, p. 186.

They Stood on the Bridge   One of the most profound lyrical folk songs in Maurice Matteson's unpublished collection. There is no listed source of this text and air found in Maurice Matteson's North Carolina mountain collection. The tune was collected circa 1936. The introduction of the piano arrangement is by Maurice Matteson and the verses are arranged for piano solo by Anthony Russell.

Blue-Eyed Ella   The text and air are from the singing of Sara Pruitt, Cleveland, South Carolina, November, 1935. This is one of several "Down in a Lonesome Valley" tunes in Maurice Matteson's collection. Maurice Matteson's original piano arrangement is adapted for piano solo by Richard L. Matteson, Jr.

Sweet Lillie   The title is a "floater" and could be also named "I'm Going to Georgia." The text and air by the singing of Nathan Hicks, Banner Elk, NC also uses "floater" verses. Maurice Matteson has arranged this tune for Soprano, Alto and Tenor. The piano solo is by Richard L. Matteson, Jr.
   For a different version, see Sharp's "I'm Going to Georgia," from EFSSA, No. 78, p. 243.

Once I Knew a Little Girl   This is one of the first tunes collected by Maurice Matteson in the Beech Mountain area. The text and air are from the singing of Nathan Hicks, Banner Elk, NC, July 1933. The piano solo is by Anthony Russell.

Star in the East   The major version of this tune is an Appalachian folk adaptation of the famous shape-note Christmas carol, "Brightest and Best." The text is from various shape-note books and the air is traditional. The shape-note versions are in a minor key. The tune is arranged by Richard L. Matteson, Jr. from his Mel Bay book, *An Appalachian Christmas.*

I Gave My Love a Cherry   Also known as "The Riddle Song," this charming text and air is from Mollye Willcox, Berea, Kentucky, circa August, 1933. This tune, from Maurice Matteson's collection, is very similar to the conventional tune used today. The piano introduction is by Maurice Matteson and the verses are arranged by Richard L. Matteson, Jr.

Sourwood Mountain   The text and air of this up-beat tune are from the singing of Zeb Dixon, Black Mountain, NC; no date given. I found this tune scribbled in Maurice Matteson's notebook. The piano arrangement is by Anthony Russell.
   For additional texts and tunes see Sharp's EFSSA No. 114, p. 312 and Wyman and Brockman's *Lonesome Tunes.*

Sinful to Flirt   The first tune collected by Maurice Matteson (see the introduction pages 00–00) in the North Carolina mountains. The text and air are from the singing of Nathan Hicks, Banner Elk, NC. The text of this tune reflects the pathos and poetic qualities of the finest Appalachian folk songs.

Barbara Allen   One of two versions found in the Maurice Matteson collection. The text and air are from the singing of Cleo Franklyn, Smyth Co., Virginia, July 14, 1934. The other version appears in *Beech Mountain Ballads.* The piano arrangement with a variation is by Cindy Long.

The Weeping Lady   From Maurice Matteson's unpublished *Three Kentucky Folk Songs for Soprano, Alto and Tenor (or SAA)* the text and air are from the singing of Mollye Wilcox, Berea, Kentucky, August 20, 1935. The arrangement for piano solo is by Maurice Matteson.

Endurance   The title and text of this tune are "floaters." The last two lines were added to complete the text which seems to be headed toward versions of "Gallis Pole," "O Judges," "Hangman." The text and air were collected by Maurice Matteson from the singing of Nathan Hicks, (listed as) Sugar Grove (?), NC. The dissonant arrangement by Maurice Matteson was adapted for piano solo by Richard L. Matteson, Jr.

It Rained   The text and air of this tune is from the singing of Mrs. J. E. Shell, Banner Elk, NC, July 15, 1933. This gem from the Maurice Matteson collection is a direct variant of the English folk song "Sir Hugh" (Child No. 155). The tune is arranged for piano solo by Ann S. Matteson and Richard L. Matteson, Jr.

The Babe of Bethlehem   The arrangement of this great shape-note Christmas carol by Richard L. Matteson, Jr. is from Mel Bay's, *An Appalachian Christmas*. The dorian melody and ballad-like text can be found in William Walker's *Southern Harmony*.

One Morning in May   This ballad was collected by Maurice Matteson on Pine Mountain, Kentucky, August 18, 1935; the singer is not known. The piano arrangement is by Richard L. Matteson, Jr.

Bow Down   This is one of two versions found in Maurice Matteson's collection. The text and air is from the singing of Hubert Brown, near Asheville, North Carolina, December 19, 1936. The piano arrangement was adapted from Maurice Matteson's original by Ann S. Matteson and Richard L. Matteson, Jr.

Willow Garden   This was collected by Maurice Matteson. The Appalachian source and date are unknown. The tune was arranged for piano solo by Anthony Russell and Richard L. Matteson, Jr.

Froggie Went a-Courtin'   This popular children's folk song was collected by Maurice Matteson. The version is different from the conventional tune of today. The tune is arranged by Maurice Matteson.
    There are many published versions of "Froggie." I like Doc Watson's version printed in Ralph Rinzler's book, *The Songs of Doc Watson*, Oak Publications 1971.

The Sheffield Apprentice   This ballad, collected by Maurice Matteson is from the singing of Mrs. William Padgett, Black Mountain, NC, July 18, 1934. The text and air are both excellent. The piano arrangement is by Ann S. Matteson and Richard L. Matteson, Jr.
    Other versions include Sharp's EFSSA No. 97, p. 278.

The Fox   A popular folk song, this version from the Maurice Matteson collection is listed as a Tennessee folk song from the singing of Grace Alder, no date given. The conventional version repeats "Den-e-o" and also repeats the last line. The piano arrangement is by Ann S. Matteson.

The Brown Girl   Also known as "Lord Thomas," this English ballad was one of the most common in the Maurice Matteson collection. The text and air are from the singing of Louisa Hubbard, Brock, Kentucky, August 16, 1933. The piano arrangement is by Richard L. Matteson, Jr.
    For other Appalachian versions of "Lord Thomas and Fair Ellinor" see Sharp's EFSSA No. 16, p. 55.

Lord Daniel   Commonly categorized as "Little Musgrave and Lady Barnard," this English ballad (Child 93) was collected by Maurice Matteson from the singing of Vivian Pike, Garrett Co., Maryland, 1940. The arrangement was adapted from Maurice Matteson's original piano version by Richard L. Matteson, Jr.

Kind Miss, I've Come A-Courtin'   Another of the frequent courtin' songs collected by Maurice Matteson. The text and air are from the singing of Cleo Franklyn, Smyth Co., Virginia, July 14, 1934. This humorous text is not found in Sharp's EFSSA and appears to be a unique song. The piano arrangement is by Richard L. Matteson, Jr.

Four Nights   A variant of "Our Goodman" (Child No. 274), this ballad is also from *Beech Mountain Ballads*" by Maurice Matteson and Melinger Henry (used by permission). The text and air are from the singing of Mrs. Mollie Hampton, Elk Park, NC, August 7, 1933. The piano arrangement is by Anthony Russell.

Sweet Willie   A variant of Earl Brand (Child No. 7), this English ballad from the Maurice Matteson collection was first published by G. Schirmer in the 1936 book, *Beech Mountain Ballads*. The text and air are from the singing of Mrs. Lloyd Bragg, Elk Park, NC, August 7, 1933. The piano arrangement is by Anthony Russell.

Bibliography

Bronson, Bertrand	*The Traditional Tunes of the Child Ballads*, Vol. 1–4, Princeton University Press, 1959–72.
Child, Francis James	*The English and Scottish Popular Ballads*, 5 vols., Houghton Mifflin Press, Boston, 1882–1889.
Matteson, Maurice with Melinger Henry	*Beech Mountain Ballads and Folksongs;* G. Schirmer and Co., New York, 1936.
	Maurice Matteson Folk Song Collection; displayed in part at The University of South Carolina and private collection.
Matteson, Richard L., Jr.	*Folk Songs from the Appalachian Mountains for Acoustic Guitar;* Mel Bay Pub., Pacific, MO, 1992.
	An Appalachian Christmas for Piano and Voice; Mel Bay Pub., Pacific, MO, 1993.
Sharp, Cecil	*English Folk Songs from the Southern Appalachians;* G. P. Putnam's Sons, New York and London, 1917.
	Eighty English Folk Songs from the Southern Appalachians, with Maud Karpeles, MIT Press, Cambridge, MA.
Warner, Frank and Anne	*Traditional American Folk Songs*, Syracuse University Press, 1984.

Great Music at Your Fingertips